KIDS SPACE
ABC Book

by Roy Jelinek

www.LittleGalileoBooks.com

Published by Little Galileo Books, LLC.
STEM & STEAM Children's Books
Pennsylvania, USA
www.LittleGalileoBooks.com

KIDS SPACE
ABC Book

by Roy Jelinek

A Asteroid

Smaller rocky, icy or metallic objects or minor planets, which orbit the sun.

B Black Hole

A stellar object possesing such great gravity, not even light can escape it.

C Comet

A small icy object orbiting the sun. It has a long glowing ion and dust tail.

D Dwarf Planet

A minor planet which has not cleared its orbit of "debris", such as Pluto.

E Earth

Planet we live on containing water oceans, and an atmosphere of oxygen.

F   Full Moon

Phase of the moon when it appears as a bright full circle in the night sky.

G Galaxy

A spiral of billions of stars, planets, dust and gas held together by gravity.

H Hubble Telescope

A space telescope orbiting the earth, which captures images of the universe.

I Ionosphere

Layer of earth's upper atmosphere containing ions and electrons.

J Jupiter

Our solar system's largest gas planet, has colored bands & a great red spot.

K　Kuiper Belt

A ring of many icy objects which lie just beyond the orbit of Neptune.

L Lunar Eclipse

As earth passes between the sun and moon, it casts a shadow on the moon.

M Meteor

A space rock which usually burns up upon entering earth's atmospere.

N Nebula

A great cloud of dust & gas in space.
It may contain many young stars.

O Orbit

Path an object takes as it moves around another object, like the sun.

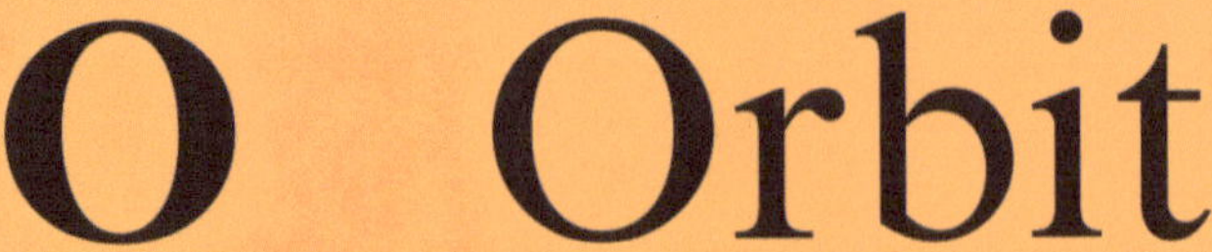

P   Pluto

Once considered the ninth planet, now reclassified as a dwarf planet.

Q Quasar

An extremely bright object that emits an enormous amount of energy.

R Rigel

One of the brightest stars in the night sky, its color is bluish-white.

S Saturn

The second largest gas giant planet in our solar system with complex rings.

T Telescope

A device used to view the light from far away objects in our universe.

U Uranus

The seventh planet, a gas giant with pale-blue color & thin ringed system.

V Venus

Bright yellow-white planet with thick atmosphere & extreme temperatures.

W   White Dwarf

Star core remains, after it exploded
and became a planetary nebula.

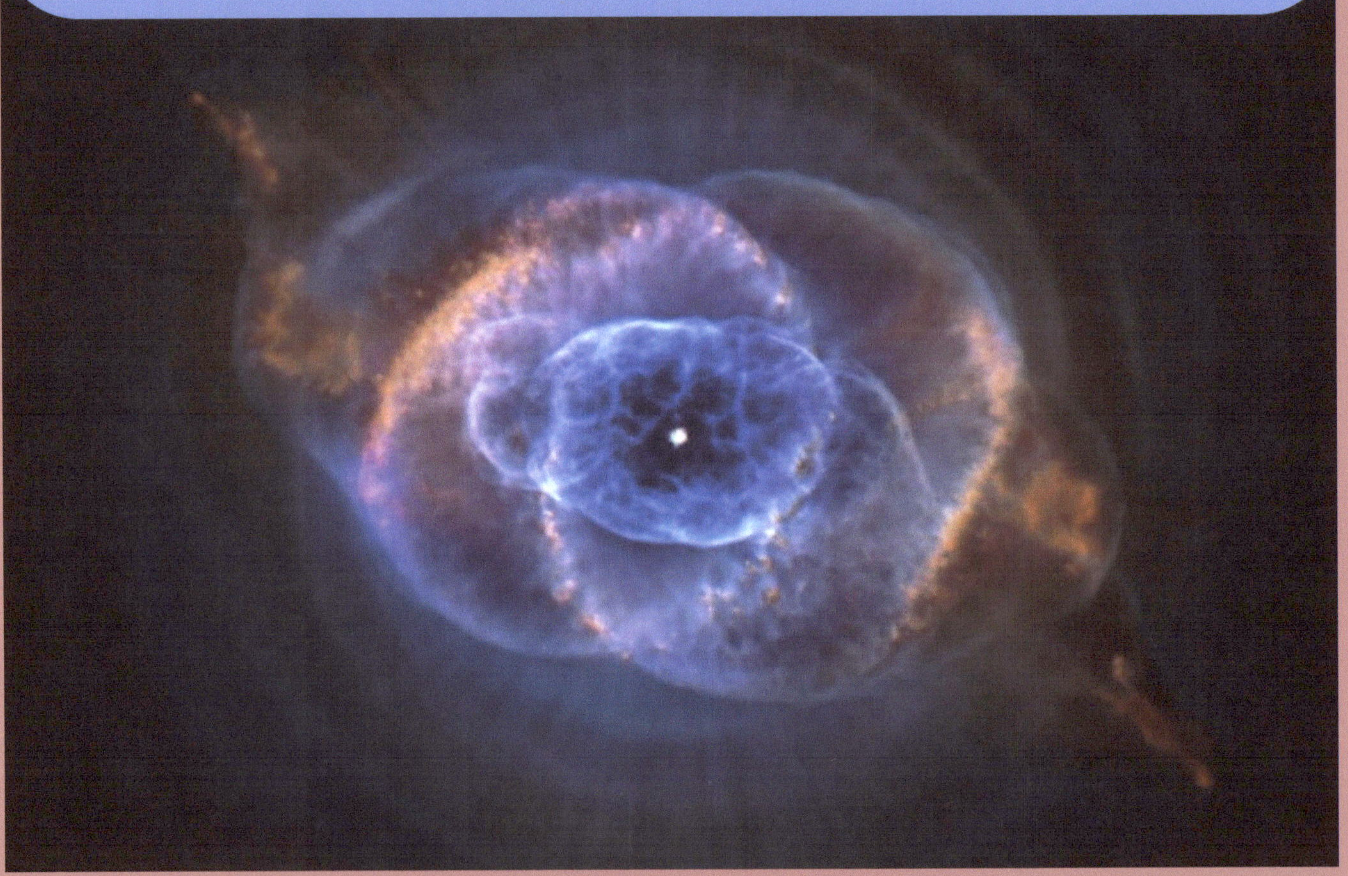

X X-ray Telescope

Space telescope that sees objects in the x-ray spectrum.

Y   Yellow Dwarf

Our sun is an example of a yellow dwarf main sequence (common) star.

Z Zodiac

The constellations that the sun passes through in its yearly movement.